For Phil
M.J.

For Mum and Dad,
Katy and Christopher,
and Mick and Keith
(for all their encouragement,
enthusiasm, and countless
cups of tea over the years)
V.W.

Text copyright © 2007 by Martin Jenkins   Illustrations copyright © 2007 by Vicky White

First U.S. edition 2007

Library of Congress Cataloging -in-Publication Data is available.

Library of Congress Catalog Card Number pending

ISBN 978-0-7636-3471-1

2 4 6 8 10 9 7 5 3 1

Printed in China

This book was typeset in Bulmer Display MT.
The illustrations were done in pencil and oil.

Candlewick Press
2067 Massachusetts Avenue
Cambridge, Massachusetts 02140

visit us at www.candlewick.com

Ape

Martin Jenkins   illustrated by Vicky White

CANDLEWICK PRESS
CAMBRIDGE, MASSACHUSETTS

There are five kinds of great apes in the world.
Each of them is different from the others . . .
but not so very different.
They're all part of the same family.

Four of them are very rare:
Orangutan, Chimp, Bonobo, Gorilla.

Here they are. . . .

Orangutan

Orangutan swings with her baby.
She has long hairy arms, with
strong hands for clutching at branches,
and feet that can grasp
the trunk of a tree.

That fruit's
out of reach . . .

Orangutans live in the rain forests of Borneo and
Sumatra in Southeast Asia. They spend almost all their time in trees.

11

but not for long.

It's a durian.

Smelly, spiky,
delicious!

Orangutans are mostly vegetarians.
They eat a lot of different kinds of fruit
but are especially fond of durians.

Orangutan looks after
her baby alone.
She keeps to herself,
high up in the treetops.

Each night she
builds a nest out of
branches to sleep on, then
pulls down a palm frond
to keep off the rain.

15

Chimp

Chimp lives in a gang

with his brothers and sisters
and uncles and cousins.

They squabble and play
and go roaming the hillsides,
hunting down monkeys
and digging up roots.

Chimpanzees
live in forests
and savannas
in central and
West Africa.

Here's a termite nest.

Chimp pokes down a hole
with a long blade of grass,
then pulls out the grass
and licks off the termites.

Chimpanzees spend a lot of
time on the ground.
They eat lots of different things
and are very good at making
and using tools.

Chimp's gang sometimes
gets into fights with
other chimp gangs—

nasty fights,
with lots of biting
and hitting.

23

Sometimes someone gets hurt.

Bonobo

Bonobo chatters and hoots

and calls to her friends,
while feasting on figs
high off the ground.

Bonobos live in the rain forest of the Congo basin in central Africa. They mostly eat different kinds of fruit.

29

She drops from the tree and
moves quickly and quietly,
watching and listening—
there may be hunters
or leopards nearby.

Bonobos spend a lot of time
feeding in the trees
but often travel on
the ground from
one feeding place
to another.

Back in the treetops,

Bonobo plays with her friends,

safe again.

Gorilla

Gorilla lounges,

chewing on bamboo stems and
chomping on leaves.

The silver hair on his back
shows that he's old.

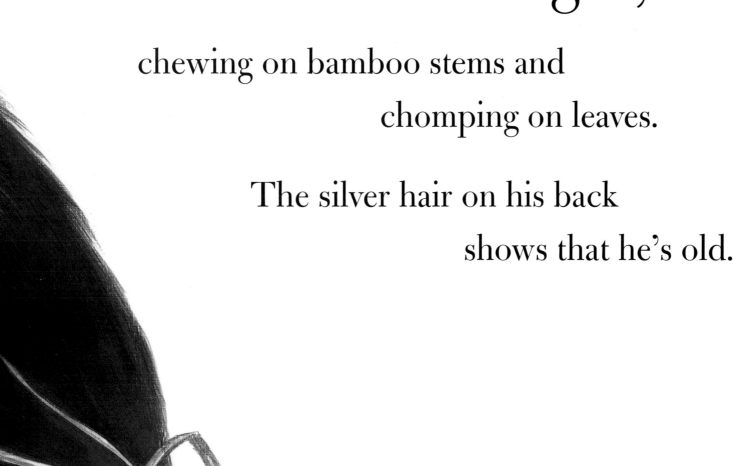

Gorillas live in the forests of central Africa.
They can get to be forty or fifty years old.

Gorilla grunts
to his family,

then snoozes.

He wakes up, plays with his baby,

then snoozes some more.

Gorillas live in small family groups of one male with a few females
and their young. They are vegetarians and spend a lot of their time eating and sleeping.

He wakes up again,
chews on some bamboo,
builds a nest for the night, and

lies down to sleep.

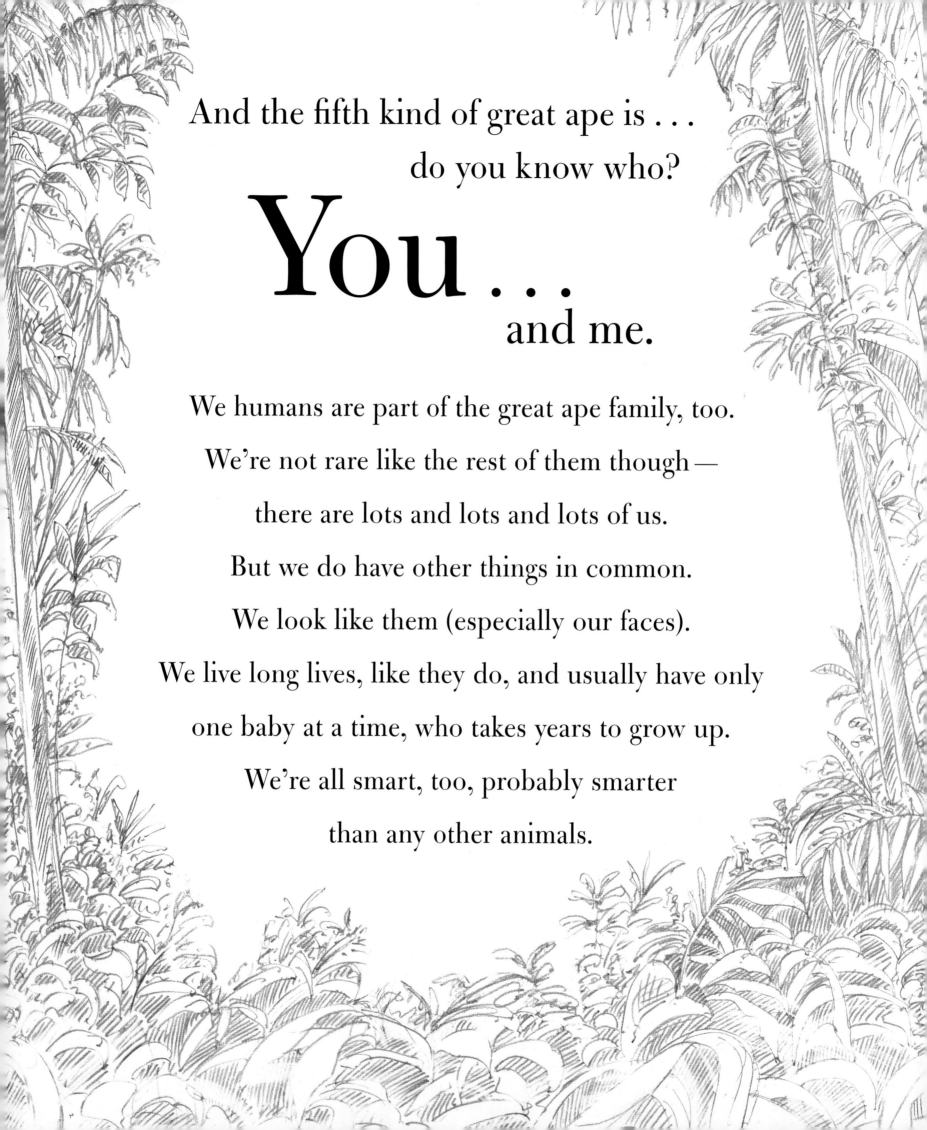

And the fifth kind of great ape is . . .

do you know who?

You . . .

and me.

We humans are part of the great ape family, too.

We're not rare like the rest of them though —

there are lots and lots and lots of us.

But we do have other things in common.

We look like them (especially our faces).

We live long lives, like they do, and usually have only

one baby at a time, who takes years to grow up.

We're all smart, too, probably smarter

than any other animals.

We're *too* smart, sometimes — at least we humans are.

We just can't stop changing things.

We've changed the world so much, we haven't

left enough room for the other great apes.

And we've hunted them — for food or to keep as pets.

In some places, though,

we're trying to protect them now.

We've set aside pieces of wild land

where they can live their lives in peace —

swinging and stomping,

chattering and playing,

eating and sleeping,

and doing all the other great things

we apes love to do!

Where the Great Apes Are

EUROPE

ASIA

AFRICA

Borneo

Sumatra

AUSTRALIA

KEY

/////////	Orangutans – *between* 50,000 *and* 80,000 *left*
═══════	Chimps – *between* 170,000 *and* 300,000 *left*
/////////	Bonobos – *between* 10,000 *and* 100,000 *left*
||||||||	Gorillas – *about* 100,000 *left*
The whole world	Humans – *more than* 6,000,000,000

These are the names and website addresses of some organizations trying to help save the great apes. (There are lots more.)

Wildlife Conservation Society – www.wcs.org
World Wildlife Fund – www.wwf.org
Conservation International – www.conservation.org